IS FOR ORISHA

by Christopher Swain

Illustrated by Victor Francisco Hernandez Mora

O is for Orisha
Copyright © 2022 Christopher Swain
By Christopher Swain
Illustrated by Victor Francisco Hernandez Mora
ISBN 9781645383987

All Rights Reserved. Written permission must be secured from the publisher to use or reproduce any part of this book, except for brief quotations in critical reviews or articles.

The divination board originally carved by Lukman Alade Fakeye was used as inspiration for the cover design.

For information, please contact:

Orange Hat Publishing
www.orangehatpublishing.com
Waukesha, WI

DEDICATION

This book is dedicated to my ancestors, those Africans who thrived happily for many years until the dreadful period in history where they were sold or stolen into the institution of slavery. Many of them perished, while others survived as human cargo in the belly of ships as they were dispersed to countries around the world, where they were either forced to practice their traditional beliefs in secret or forsake those beliefs for the belief system of their captors. Thank you to all my spiritual teachers and guides for embracing me and sharing your time, wisdom, knowledge, and love. I also dedicate this book to my global family—past, present, and future—to remind them of our traditional beliefs before the ships came and to reawaken the African within. I would especially like to acknowledge and thank the Orishas, Orisas, and Orixas for their continued guidance and inspiration in my daily life.

WHAT IS AN ORISHA?

According to the ancient Ifa belief system practiced amongst the people of Yorubaland, an Orisha is a spirit placed on earth to help humans in our daily lives. Olodumare (God) the creator, is responsible for their existence and the specific duties of each Orisha. It's estimated that there are 401 or more Orishas. They are Olodumare's oldest children, and each reflects an aspect of nature. They are the mediator between the creator and humans.

As African people were enslaved and carried away to distant lands, so was this belief. The belief soon evolved to survive alongside the religion of the colonizers. In lands where Catholicism was practiced, the Yoruba people secretly aligned each Orisha with a specific Roman Catholic saint. The original praise or worship day for each Orisha changed also because the Yoruba calendar only has four (4) days. Each Orisha also has specific numbers, colors, and associated symbols that they represent. Today, the Ifa belief system is widely practiced and has given birth to other belief systems and religions all over the world.

ESU

My name is Esu and I'm an Orisha! I am the first Orisha created by Olodumare. I'm sometimes called the trickster. I'm the owner of the crossroads and doorways.

I'm present everyplace decisions must be made. I am the master of all languages. I'm the Divine Messenger and gateway through which all prayers and requests to the Orishas must pass.

I enjoy toys, silver coins, and keys. My favorite treats are cigars, candy and coconuts.

My colors are red and black, and my number is 3 (three) and multiples of 3 (three). My day of the week is Monday. My symbols are a straw hat and a hooked stick.

"Saint Anthony"

OBATALA

My name is Obatala and I'm an Orisha! I am king of the white cloth and all things that are white. I am the son of Olodumare who gave me the job of creating the earth and humans. I'm also the father of many Orishas.

I always wear white clothing as a symbol of my cool energy and pure spirit. I enjoy cotton, snails, cocoa butter, and white rice.

My color is white, and my number is 8 (eight). My days of the week are Sunday and Thursday. My symbols are snail shells, ivory, mountains, white animals, and silver and other white metals.

"Our Lady of Mercy"

ORUNMILA

My name is Orunmila and I'm an Orisha! I am the Orisha of divination. I was there when Olodumare created the universe. I know the future of everyone.

I know everything about your life from the beginning to the end. I communicate with humans through a Babalawo using a divination board. I enjoy coconuts, candles, and cakes.

My colors are yellow and green. My number is 16 (sixteen) and my day of the week is Sunday. My symbols are the palm nut, cowrie shells, and a divination board that I always carry with me.

"Saint Francis of Assisi"

My name is Osun and I'm an Orisha! I am the youngest of all Orishas. I am the Orisha of love and sweetness. In nature, I rule rivers that sustain life. I am the sweetness of life.

I represent beauty, love, and courage. There is a festival to celebrate me every year. I love silks, perfumes, fans, mirrors, and all kinds of jewelry, especially gold, brass, coral, and amber. My favorite treat is honey and I love sunflowers.

My colors are yellow and gold. My number is 5 (five) and multiples of 5 (five). My day of the week is Saturday. My symbols are parrots, peacocks, and vultures.

"Our Lady of Charity"

SHANGO

My name is Shango and I'm an Orisha! I am the Orisha of drumming, dancing, male beauty, and passion. In nature I rule thunder, lightning, and fire. I'm the son of Yemoja. I was the original owner of the divination board before I traded it to Orunmila in exchange for the sacred bata drums.

I'm also a powerful sorcerer who can spit fire. Each year after the festival to celebrate Osun, there is a festival held in honor of me also. I love music, okra, bananas, and women.

My number is 6 (six) and my day of the week is Friday. My symbols are the single and double-headed axe and thunderstones.

"Saint Barbara"

OYA

My name is Oya and I'm an Orisha! I am the Orisha of change and the marketplace. I rule the winds, storms, and tornadoes. I am the cause of change in nature and in life. I don't destroy anything that is necessary. I'm also the gatekeeper of cemeteries.

I'm always seen wearing a skirt of 9 (nine) different colors representing each of my children. I enjoy grapes, eggplants, and white rice. I also enjoy copper bangle bracelets.

My colors are purple, burgundy, red, and orange. My number is 9 (nine) and my day of the week is Friday. My symbols are a black flywhisk made from the tail of a horse, masks, and machetes.

"Saint Theresa"

OGUN

My name is Ogun and I'm an Orisha! I am the Orisha of all iron and metal. I'm the patron Orisha of blacksmiths, policemen, mechanics, surgeons, and all who work with metal.

I can be found at railroad tracks and in the forests and wilderness. I enjoy kola nuts, roasted sweet potatoes, and palm oil.

My colors are green and black. My numbers any combinations of 3 (three) or 7 (seven). My days of the week are Tuesday and Wednesday. My symbols are railroad tracks, hammer, shovel, and all metal tools.

"Saint Peter"

YEMOJA

My name is Yemoja and I'm an Orisha! I rule the seas and can be found in all waters. I live in the part of the ocean that gives life to the world, where fish, plants, and many other sea creatures dwell.

I love anything related to the sea like fish, sea horses, seashells, oars, and boat anchors. I also enjoy dancing while wearing my long blue and white skirt. I'm the Orisha of pregnant women.

My colors are blue and clear. My number is 7 (seven) and my day of the week is Saturday. My symbols are boats, anchors, oars, and fish.

"Our Lady of Regla"

BABALU AYE

My name is Babalu Aye and I'm an Orisha! I rule over all the diseases in the world of which I can both deliver and cure. I'm sometimes called the Orisha of smallpox. Sometimes when uncontrollable and angry, I spread diseases as punishment for wasteful and unreasonable living.

I am also the guardian and protector of the poor. I'm usually seen walking with a cane or crutch with 2 (two) dogs by my side. I enjoy popcorn, rum, cigars, and beans.

My colors are brown earth tones, purple, blue, and black. My number is 17 (seventeen) and my days of the week are Sunday and Wednesday. My symbols are crutches.

"Saint Lazarus"

IBEJI

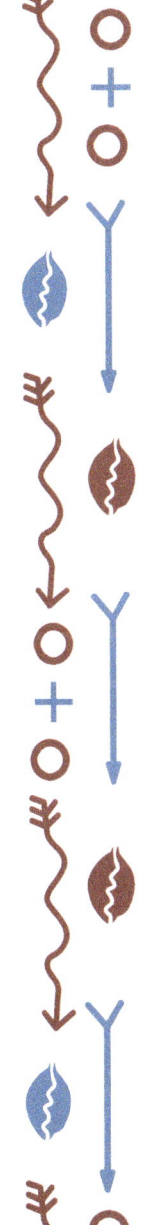

We are Ibeji and we are an Orisha! We are one soul that lives in two bodies. We are the Orisha of twins and all things in pairs. We represent joy, abundance, laughter, and all things childlike.

We were the first twins born on earth to our parents Shango and Osun, but we were raised by Oya. I'm Taiwo, the first born yet youngest of the twins and I'm always seen wearing red. I'm Kehinde, the second born yet oldest of the twins and I'm always seen wearing blue. We enjoy sweet foods, and our day of the week is Sunday.

Our numbers are 2 (two), 4 (four), and 8 (eight) and our colors are red and blue. Our symbols are pairs of wooden dolls and palm trees.

"Saint Cosme and Damian"

OSHOSI

My name is Oshosi and I'm an Orisha! I am the Orisha of hunting and justice. In the forests I'm a master hunter and never miss my target.

I'm also a wizard who's closely associated with Ogun and Esu. I enjoy all types of hunted wild animals including birds. Bananas, grapes, pears, and pomegranates are also enjoyable to me.

My colors are blue and amber. My numbers are 3 (three) and 7 (seven). My days of the week are Monday and Wednesday. My symbols are a crossbow and arrow.

"Saint Nobert"

OSHUMARE

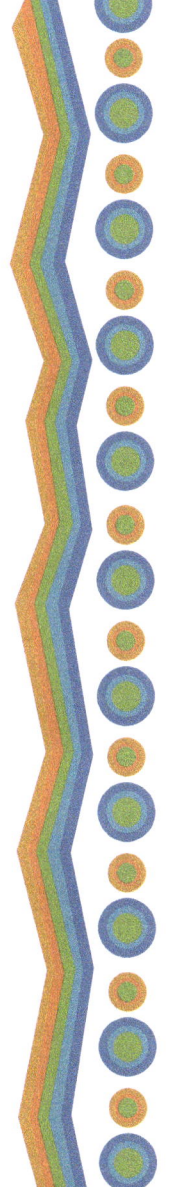

My name is Oshumare and I'm an Orisha! I'm the Orisha of transformation, cycles and movement. I represent the union of heaven and earth as well as balance and unity.

When you see a rainbow, you're looking at me as a snake of many colors stretched across the sky, which represents blessings for humanity. I enjoy coconut, duck, flowers, and water.

My colors are yellow, green, and pink. My numbers are 7 (seven) and 12 (twelve). My days of the week are Sunday and Tuesday. My symbol is a rainbow-colored snake.

"Saint Bartholomew"

OLOKUN

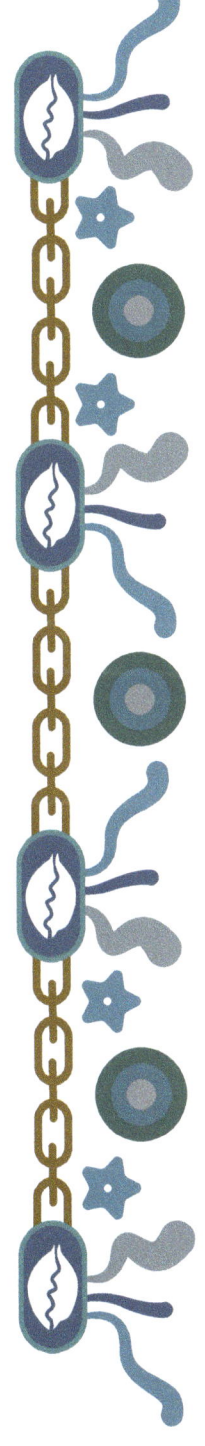

My name is Olokun and I'm an Orisha! I live in the deepest parts of the ocean where no man can reach. I rule all waters of the earth. I'm the owner of seas, also known as the Orisha of deep mysteries and dark secrets.

I'm easily identified by my half human / half fish appearance and the mask that I sometimes wear or carry. I love all fruits of the earth.

My colors are dark blue and off white. My numbers are 7 (seven) and 9 (nine). My day of the week is Monday. My symbol is the mudfish which lives both in water and on land.

OSAYIN

My name is Osayin and I'm an Orisha! I'm the owner and ruler of all plants and herbs. I live in the forest where I watch over the plants. Since traditional medicines are made from plants, I'm considered to be a healing Orisha.

Ase, the force of the universe is believed to come from plants. Due to my knowledge of plants, I can activate their Ase. I'm also a powerful wizard and I keep this magic hanging from a tall tree inside of a calabash. I'm easily recognized because I'm small and walk with a cane because I have one hand, one foot, and one of my ears is very small. I enjoy water, gin, and all plants.

I'm represented by many colors. My numbers are 7 (seven) and 21 (twenty-one) and my day of the week is Sunday.

"Saint Sylvester"

ERINLE

My name is Erinle and I'm an Orisha! I'm both a hunter/fisherman and healer on land and sea where I represent the gifts of both through hunting and fishing. I'm a water spirit.

I live both in the forests and in water in the space where the sweet river meets the salty ocean. I'm always seen with my fishing hook and staff dressed in fine fabrics covered with coral beads, cowrie shells, and snakes wrapped around my body. I enjoy art, music, cooked plantains, and wine.

My colors are turquoise blue and coral or blue, white, and yellow. My day of the week is Tuesday, and my number is 7. My symbols are fish and fishing rods.

"Saint Raphael"

OBBA

My name is Obba and I'm an Orisha! I'm the Orisha of ponds, marriage, home, lakes, and guardian of graves. I live in the cemetery. I'm the daughter of Yemoja. I rule the Obba River in Nigeria. I was the first wife of Shango.

I'm also a great cook. I taught the Orishas how to read and write. I love all types of jewelry, which I keep in a special box. Due to a terrible trick, I'm now missing one of my ears. I enjoy water from ponds or lakes, wine, flowers, and candles.

My colors are burgundy and pink. My number is 8 (eight) and my days of the week are Sunday and Friday. My symbols are burgundy or pink flowers and interlocking wedding rings.

"Saint Catherine of Sienna"

OZUN

My name is Ozun and I'm an Orisha!
I am the messenger of Obatala.
I'm the guardian who protects you
and never sleeps.

I will warn you of any dangers.
I represent stability and good health.
I enjoy sweet fruits and cigars.

I have no special color because I am present in all colors. I'm represented by a white metal rooster, dove, or dog seated upon a tall pedestal cup. My number is 8 (eight) and multiples of 8 (eight). My day of the week is Thursday. My symbol is the white dove.

"Saint John the Baptist"

AGANJU

My name is Aganju and I'm an Orisha! I'm the Orisha of the wilderness and deserts. Outside of Nigeria, I'm also the Orisha of volcanoes. I create new land with lava from volcanoes and with the sand and dirt moved by rivers into new places.

I own all minerals of the earth. As a navigator whose skill is exploring unknown territories, I'm the ferryman that helps people across the rivers. I enjoy rooster, mangos, bananas, okra, and pigeons.

My colors are brown and opal. My number is 9 (nine) and my day of the week is Friday. My symbol is a double-headed axe with two curved handles.

"Saint Christopher"

GLOSSARY

ASE - divine force that is the essence of God.

BABALAWO - father of mysteries, priest of Orunmila or a traditional healer in West Africa.

BATA DRUM - an hourglass shaped drum with 3 heads on each end used primarily in religious ceremonies.

COWRIE – a group of small to large snail shells used as money or offerings in West Africa.

DIVINATION – a method of seeking spiritual guidance and knowledge known only by trained individuals.

IFA – divination system of the Yoruba people. Religion of the Yoruba people.

KOLA NUT – the bitter seed of a kola tree often used in Ifa ceremonies.

NIGERIA – a country located on the west coast of Africa bordered by Cameroon, Benin, and Niger. The highest populated country in Africa.

OLODUMARE – supreme creator God.

ORISHA – also spelled Orisa and Orixa; spiritual deities that guide and govern our daily lives

YORUBA – ethnic group of African people originated in Yorubaland (Nigeria, Benin, and Togo). Spoken language of Yoruba people.

AUTHOR

Photo Credit: Melissa "Phyllis Iller" Alexander

Christopher Swain was born in Atlanta, Georgia where he is an avid collector of Tribal African Art and artifacts from various cultures. Christopher is passionate about Africa and her countless contributions to the world and spent the last 25+ years visiting countries such as Egypt, Cote d'Ivoire, Cameroon, Mali, Burkina Faso, Kenya, Ghana, South Africa, Ethiopia, Tanzania, Niger, Rwanda, Togo, Senegal, Nigeria, Morocco, Benin, Zimbabwe, Botswana, Jamaica, Brazil, and Cuba attending various cultural festivals, celebrations, and sacred spiritual ceremonies.

ILLUSTRATOR

Photo Credit: JoGo Art "Jose Gonzalez"

Victor Francisco Hernandez Mora was born in Havana, Cuba where he is a painter, illustrator, graphic artist, and a muralist. Victor has displayed his work in more than 20 personal exhibitions both inside and outside of Cuba. Victor Mora has illustrated 7 books/projects, including being distinguished as the only Cuban artist in the history of art itself, to illustrate a version of the Holy Bible that was published in Mexico.

www.ingramcontent.com/pod-product-compliance
Lightning Source LLC
LaVergne TN
LVHW070949070426
835507LV00029B/3461